Making Art Special

A Curriculum for Special

Education Art

Helen Goren Shafton

Acknowledgments

I extend my gratitude to my sister, Irene Redman, who took the time and energy to edit my manuscript with a fine-toothed comb. I cannot thank my husband Jack enough for his insights, encouragement and support for this project. Thanks to my sons, Jason and Jeremy, for their support and for helping me with all things computer-related. Thank you to Dr. Heather Fountain, of Kutztown University, for generously sharing her wisdom with me and opening my eyes to the importance of language that puts people first. Thanks also to Jane McKeag and the staff at Davis Publications for pointing me in the right direction. Many thanks also to the special education team at Park View Elementary School in Glen Ellyn, Illinois. Without the help of my principal, the teachers and instructional assistants, this book would not have been possible. They were there in the trenches with me as I developed and implemented these lessons. I also want to send a special thank you to the students in the Guided Instruction Program who taught me much more than I could ever teach them. They are my inspiration and my joy.

Making Art Special

Table of Contents

Making Art Special

Introduction

Welcome and hold on tight, because I am tossing you the equivalent of an educational lifeline. If you are an art teacher, classroom teacher, special educator, physical therapist, caregiver or parent of a child with disabilities, you have found a resource that I would have jumped for joy to discover a few years ago.

In the fall of 2006 my elementary art teaching responsibilities expanded to include two small groups of six students with disabilities. My usual load of classes includes a total of approximately 550 students in two schools each week. Keeping everyone's names straight was my biggest challenge to that point. Well, perhaps I am oversimplifying, because managing materials, resources and my time was certainly challenging as well. However, when it came to planning and delivering curriculum and instruction, I knew what I was doing. That all changed when I prepared for my first class with these students who had a variety of cognitive, motor and speech disabilities. Or should I say when I was ill-prepared to work with these students? Over the years I had coursework in special education and I had worked with students who had IEPs (Individual Education Plans). However, I had never been given the responsibility to plan and implement art lessons on a weekly basis to students who were non-verbal, could not apply consistent pressure with their hands, could not cut with a scissors and, in some cases, could not keep art materials out of their mouths. This was new. This was enough to send me into my principal's office looking for help!

Armed with the confidence of my principal and my lifelong attitude that any new problem can be solved by a little research, I set out to find some resources. I looked for examples of self-contained, special education art programs in my community to observe, and learn from experienced professionals. There were none. I looked for graduate classes on the subject to no avail.

In order to provide these children with expressive, experiential opportunities that all of my first through fifth graders have, I needed to develop open-ended activities that inspire creative thinking, self-discovery and an expanded worldview. I did not want to make "cookie-cutter art" projects that all look the same. Finally I decided to do what I often do when I need to learn something . . . I went to the library. I found many books with arts and crafts projects for preschoolers and young children, but I did not find any books that would provide me with authentic art experiences for elementary students with disabilities. I found one interesting book intended for preschoolers, *Young at Art,* by Susan Striker, which presents some wonderful exploratory ideas for working with color, shape, line, and various art concepts in combination with music, games, food and literature. This inspired me to begin by simply providing these students with opportunities to freely explore a wide range of art materials without any rules. Much of what younger students make in the regular classroom is very structured, often with right and wrong ways to assemble something, such as a fire truck. These activities are important to their development and understanding of the world around them, but I wanted to give them the opportunity to choose what they wanted to use and how they wanted to use it. And thus began the challenge of developing weekly lessons through trial and error. Fortunately for me, I have had only a handful of what I would call an error, and I have learned a great deal from those lessons myself!

This journey into providing art education to a unique population has made me look at myself and my teaching in new ways because every class has students with a variety of abilities. Also a wonderful outcome of this experience is that I am no longer searching for an experienced professional in my community as a resource. I have become that art teacher, who wants to help others on this journey into providing art experiences for everyone. I hope this resource helps you face the challenges in your work or family life with a newfound confidence.

Connecting the Dots

As far back as the 1950s educational researchers have published books that should be mentioned here in order to gain some perspective on the subject of art education, the brain and students with disabilities. In addition, education laws have changed dramatically, affecting who and how we teach.

Lowenfeld's (1957) book, *Creative and Mental Growth,* described the art process as promoting self-expression, independence, flexible thinking, social interactions and general well being. Again in the 1950s and later in the 70s, Kramer (1971) pointed to the therapeutic aspects of art experiences, while emphasizing the growth of skills and an aesthetic awareness. Also during the 1950s, the classification of the affective domain of the brain was elaborated by Krathwohl, Bloom & Masia (1956) and involves receiving, responding, valuing, and organizing. This domain is driven by the feelings or willingness of the student. In contrast, the cognitive domain involves knowledge, comprehension, application, analysis, synthesis, and evaluation. If we connect the dots here and put Lowenfeld's and Kramer's knowledge of the positive affect of art on the well being of the student in the context of connecting the cognitive and affective domains (Krathwohl, Bloom, Masia) then we can see the link between the art process and learning in a way that is both unique and important to the child with disabilities. Through art, we can provide children with disabilities an opportunity to learn about themselves, as well as the world around them, with open-ended experiences that build on cognitive skills and promote self-expression and well being.

We have come a long way when we consider that prior to the Education for All Handicapped Children Act of 1975, many children with developmental challenges were routinely institutionalized. This Act did not directly refer to art education as a core subject required by law. It was mentioned as a "related service" (Gerber & Guay, 2006) along with music and dance. Suddenly there was a mainstreaming of thousands of students with disabilities, and teachers were faced with the task of providing instruction without adequate funding or training. For the art teacher, the therapeutic benefits of art education, as suggested by Lowenfeld and Kramer, provided these students with avenues for success and self-expression. According to Gerber and Guay, art teachers "opened the door to broader mainstreaming efforts." (2006, p.19) Today we find a range of placements for students with disabilities including: full time mainstreaming in general education classes; part-time placement in special education classes; and, full-time, self-contained special education classes. Regardless of placement, we know that art has a unique impact on the total child.

The idea of art as therapy is not an appropriate approach for the art educator. A trained art therapist seeks an understanding of the psychological dynamics of the individual through art. An art educator encourages the self-expression of the child through art. We can, however, adapt our lessons to combine the therapeutic benefits of the art process with the promotion of the intellectual, aesthetic, social and psychological growth of the child (Henley, 1992).

For a detailed overview of special education laws I would recommend the chapter dedicated to the subject in the book *Reaching and Teaching Students with Special Needs through Art,* by Gerber and Guay (2006).

Getting Started

Getting yourself ready to meet the demands of providing art instruction to students with disabilities requires some information, some helpers and some classroom management preparation. Here are some steps I wish I had considered before I got started . . .

Know Your Audience

Students with IEPs (Individual Education Plans) are like other students in that they have strengths and areas to improve. For my elementary students with disabilities the areas to improve are often more basic in nature such as learning to write their own names or cut on a line. Given the appropriate information at the beginning, planning lessons for these students is much easier. The first thing to do is ask the classroom teacher for a copy of the student's IEP. In addition to the IEP, I also recommend asking the teacher to provide a very brief list of each student's strengths and areas to improve. These jewels of information guide lesson planning and assessment of student progress. Of course your own observations are going to be critical to figuring out each child's abilities and needs. According to Wong (2004), the first interactions he has with his students are spent observing, identifying and evaluating student behaviors, abilities and personalities. Notes from these first encounters are the basis for creating successful learning experiences for all students.

It is my goal to design each lesson to reinforce learning in and practice of multiple areas in need of improvement for the students. Each lesson is assessed based upon each student's demonstration of understanding or achievement in multiple areas in need of improvement. I will provide more information about developing lessons and assessment of student performance later in the text.

An Octopus Would Be Handy

Unless you are an octopus, you are going to need some extra hands. Sometimes the ratio of adults per students in special education classes is good, but not always. I have been fortunate to have as many as three adults with me for six or seven students. We can do this together. We put on our aprons, and we get to work! If you do not have adequate adult help, you may want to ask for some art buddies from the older student population. Extra hands can have had a tremendous impact on the success of the program for your students with disabilities.

Whether you have adult instructional assistants or student art buddies, you need to meet with them and express your desire to provide the students with artistic opportunities that allow them to make decisions and try to do things for themselves. You can provide a written list of objectives for the lesson, or this information can be shared informally at the beginning of class. Good communication between the art teacher and the instructional assistants is very important to the success of the lesson and the overall positive atmosphere in the art room. There will be times when it is apparent that a child needs help with cutting, gluing or some other task. It is important for the instructional assistants to understand when and how to help, as well as when to let the student work on their own. In order to encourage decision-making, risk taking, independence and self-expression, the student needs to select materials and decide how/where to use them. For example, if using a scissors presents a challenge for the student, it would be useful to take turns helping the student and letting him try it alone. If a student is gluing pieces of fabric down on a collage, she should decide what fabric to use and where to put it. This is the part of art-making that has to do with self-expression and decision-making, so it would not be helpful to select the fabric pieces for the students or to make glue dots for them without asking where they want to glue the fabric. When coloring, it is fun to color along with the students. They love to see what we adults can do, but we can do that on our own paper. Coloring the project for the student does not provide him with an opportunity for self-expression. Helping them to hold the crayon or pencil so students can express themselves may sometimes be necessary using a simple hand-over-hand technique. It is important to distinguish between helping and doing it for them.

A Few Words about Classroom Management

Start with a complete plan to manage the students. The special education teacher can help you formulate this plan based on the students' behavior plans and successful methods used in the classroom. It is very important that you are comfortable with these methods. If not, you probably will not use them which will leave you without a plan. I suggest a reward system such as a sticker chart that can be displayed for each child, in addition to the immediate gratification of a small edible treat and free choice activities. The sticker chart is a visual reminder of past performance and the promise of future praise. The treat has an immediate positive effect. The free choice activities serve multiple functions. The children enjoy themselves, practice how to play together or independently and, depending upon the activities, they are learning. I like to collect sturdy, large, colorful books and puzzles for these students as well as interesting toys with which to manipulate or build. Playdoh is always a fun option. Another free choice activity that is very popular is watercolor painting, which is a very relaxing and pleasurable activity. Providing a free choice activity board or cards that illustrate their choices helps students make a selection when they have earned this reward.

What do you do if a student refuses to participate, or follow directions or lies on the floor in a limp heap? I would not recommend trying to drag or lift a student. This can be psychologically negative for the child and physically hard on you. Instead, it is best to give the student a reminder of his choices, the reward system, and the consequences of behavior not worthy of a reward. In my experience, the students are typically interested in what we are making; however, occasionally someone acts out during art class. In order to manage these counterproductive behaviors the emphasis needs to be on allowing the student the opportunity to listen to her options and make a good choice. For example, you could suggest, "you can come back to the table and do your work or you can stay there on the floor. If you do your work you will get free choice time with _____(insert favorite free choice item here), a sticker and a treat. If you do not do your work you will not get a sticker, etc." Clearly explaining the choices and allowing the student a few moments to make the right choice usually works. Then you can praise the good decision.

Sometimes you may need an alternate activity provided by the classroom teacher, which can be referred to as a "working time out". This can be a time when the student sits alone and has sorting to do. Such a neutral, structured activity can help steer the child back to a more cooperative frame of mind. Figure out

11

these plans in advance. Ask the classroom teacher what motivates the students. Prepare your reward system, such as a sticker chart, treat and alternate activity for working time outs. You will feel ready to manage your classroom. In the most extreme situations in which a student is behaving in an uncontrollable fashion or is violent to others or self, the student may have to be escorted back to the classroom to calm down. Discuss this plan with the teacher and instructional assistants in advance so you are all prepared for this in the event it is necessary.

Preparing Your Room for the Students and the Students for Your Room

The art room is an amazing, visually stimulating place filled a variety of materials that your students should <u>not</u> touch for their own safety and for the protection of other students' artwork. Therefore, here are a few suggestions to prepare your classroom.

First, think about safety. If your room is disorganized, you will have to clean it up. Organize your room so there is a large area that is free of dangerous materials and objects and can be open to the movement of your students. Limiting use of the room to one small area can be challenging. The instructional assistants or art buddies can help monitor student movement to keep them and the other students' art projects safe.

Second, introduce the idea of coming to the art room and behaving appropriately through the use of a Social Story. Social Stories are books created to explain something new to students with disabilities. These books are particularly useful with students on the Autism spectrum, but they also work well with any group that struggles with change or transitions. I photographed the entire process associated with going to the art classroom and making art, which resulted in a Social Story that included photos of: the students lined up at their classroom door, the art room door, me in my apron, their table in the art room, art supplies, students working at a table, the sink for cleaning up, free choice activities, rewards, and students lined up to leave the art room. The caption for each picture was simple and brief, such as "It's time for art. Let's line up at the door." The pages can be laminated and bound together. When I transitioned my students into the art room from their classroom, I used the book to help the process along. The best part was when we finished reading the book and actually went to the room for a tour. The students demonstrated that they remembered what they had heard about in the Social Story. When we walked into the art room, they sat down at their table without being asked! That made me smile. After our tour, we visited the art room a few more times. Once we came into the room and read the Social Story again. The next time we encouraged the students to take individual tours of the room and look at materials up close. On the last visit we did a small activity and the following week the students were ready to come to the art room for an entire class period. This gradual transition was suggested by the special educators in my building and proved to be very effective. The professionals in your building can be an excellent resource to guide you through this process.

Finally, be prepared! Have your supplies ready. Troubleshoot your lesson, as suggested by Gerber and Guay (2006). Consider the seating arrangements, the appropriateness of the materials you are using, the simplicity of the directions and the vocabulary you will be using. Taking the time to think through these important factors can help identify potential problems and lead to success for your students. Test your lesson to make sure it is well thought out. Have a couple of lessons ready, because some students can move through activities more quickly than expected. Have the free choice activities ready, so you can transition smoothly.

Adaptive Art Supplies

Depending on the particular challenges facing your students, you will probably need some different art supplies. For example, there are some suppliers who offer special spring loaded scissors that will be helpful to students who have difficulties with fine motor skills. There are also rolling scissors that are safe and can be very helpful. Chubby crayons, pencils and brushes are excellent for students with fine motor limitations, as well as universal cuffs with Velcro to assist with holding supplies. A variety of stencils are great for students to use alone or with assistance to help them create their desired shapes. Check with the special educator and physical/occupational therapist in your building for suggestions on what supplies would be beneficial to the students in your art program. Also, you can investigate the Additional Resources at the end of this text for adaptive supplies.

Developmental Stages and Drawing

Typical lesson planning for art must take into consideration the developmental stages of children.   Lowenfeld (1964) describes the stages as follows: At two years of age typically children are scribbling. By age three to four they are considered pre-schematic, meaning their first forms are general symbols for a constantly changing conceptualization of the world around them. Some of their schema is more recognizable than others. By age six children reach the schematic stage in which their drawing better represents their world. Objects sit on a baseline, showing no concept of depth. Age eight to ten is typically the dawn of realism, where specific schema are developed, detailed and overlapped, showing a sense of depth and space. To further our understanding of child development, we can look to Edward's book, *Drawing on the Right Side of the Brain* (1999), which presents a more refined version of Lowenfeld's stages. Children emerge from scribbling to general, circular symbols for everything by age three, which leads to story pictures to work out feelings or problems by age four or five. By age six, a child's basic landscape develops, with a blue line and sun at the top and a green line at the bottom. By age nine or ten he develops a complexity of detail and realism, as Lowenfeld suggests, but the child is concerned with how things really look rather than where they are located.

Due to the varied challenges faced by your students with disabilities these stages do not necessarily occur as described by Lowenfeld and others. It is necessary to look at your students' unique sets of strengths and areas to improve. Take into consideration the development of your students and go back to the beginning stages. Scribbling is a very pleasant, sensory experience. Let your students scribble with a variety of materials on a variety of surfaces. Using white pencil on black paper, for example, is a very interesting change from the usual drawing materials on white paper. Drawings can be combined, compared and discussed. Moving on to drawing symbols, general circles or representative schema may not be something your students are ready to do. Stencils can be very helpful with these students. Working with stencils requires eyes focused on the task and many muscles controlling the hand. Using stencils may not be something your students can do by themselves.   Try large containers to trace around first before trying large stencils. Put a thicker-bodied pencil in the child's hand and place your hand over hers to assist. For those who can make symbols, encourage them to make more symbols over time. Provide different drawing tools to encourage their fine motor refinement. Teach them to repeat their symbols to create patterns. You can demonstrate some symbols that can be used to develop a basic landscape, such as house, sun, grass and tree. This will aid students on the Autism spectrum to find order in their world, which can lead to contentment and peace of mind.

For those who like to write words instead of drawing a symbol, try drawing a very basic symbol such as the sun or a flower, and ask them what it is. Invite them to write the word. Then reverse the process: you write the word and ask them to draw a symbol. Keep it simple, so their confidence remains strong and they are willing to participate. For those who do not want to draw, try painting....

Thoughts on Painting

Start with thicker-handled paintbrushes, lots of newspaper and watercolor paint sets. Use thicker papers that can handle lots of water. Reminding the students to dip the brush into the paint, not the just the water, is important. Later, you can add different papers, paints and additives to the paint. Over time, you can teach them to clean their brushes in the water between colors. Some students have difficulty using a container of water without spilling, so a good substitute is spraying the paint tray with a water bottle to moisten all of the colors or use a shallow pan of water, instead of a taller container. For students who have stronger fine motor skills, using a small brush can lead to some amazing, detailed results. Initially, just let them enjoy this relaxing, sensory experience. Painting is my students' favorite activity, which is why it is one of our free choice activities. Using a variety of paints such as glitter paint or acrylic paint on a variety of surfaces adds to the enjoyment!

Thoughts on Printmaking

Printmaking is a technique that always yields a wonderful response from students when they first see it. As a printmaker myself, I have experienced that sense of wonder again and again as I have continued making prints for decades! If you have never made a print before, this is something you will want to experiment with in advance of doing it with students. It is important to have water-based inks when working with children. The oil-based varieties make a much bigger mess that is not necessary to the process. Covering yourself and your workspace is a good start. Students can wear smocks.

You can make prints with almost anything, such as using a piece of Styrofoam from a grocery store meat tray. Cut a small rectangle of the Styrofoam to use as your printing block and use a pencil to draw lines, shapes or any image you like. If you are using words, you will need to write backwards.

You will need a flat, non-porous surface, such as a cookie sheet or large piece of heavyweight plastic or acrylic, for rolling out the ink. Squeeze a small amount at first and roll out the ink using an ink brayer (or roller). This tool is very different from a paint roller in that it is also non-porous and very hard. By rolling the ink back and forth repeatedly the ink is smooth and ready for use. The more you roll it the smoother and drier it becomes, so experiment with how much rolling is required in order to make the ink smooth and ready, but still moist. Once your printing block is ready to print, roll ink over it, making the entire surface wet with ink. Carefully lay the paper on top of your inked design and hold it still with one hand while rubbing gently with the other hand. This is a very important step. If the paper moves, the print will be ruined with a double image. Lift the paper and enjoy the exciting results. Be sure to keep the ink fresh, adding more as needed for each additional print. Printmaking is so much fun. You can use various textured materials for printmaking, and my lessons include a few ideas.

Designing Lessons

When designing lessons, it is important to first consider the students' abilities, various ways to engage the senses, and the National or State Standards. In an art class with students who are high functioning, more art appreciation and discussion is possible, therefore the lesson will be tailored to fit the group's ability to focus on stimuli and discuss it. Engaging the senses will engage the mind and help encourage growth and reduce off-task behavior. Aligning with recognized standards is important to establishing the art program as "rigorous [and] rich...not fluff...a program that leaves no child behind in art." (Passmore, 2005)

Assignments and assessments can be adjusted in an effort to differentiate to meet the needs of all students.   According to Tomlinson (1999), teachers can use an equalizer or series of continuums to adjust the challenge level based upon student readiness. There are nine continuums as outlined by Tomlinson: foundational to transformational, concrete to abstract, simple to complex, single facet to multiple facets, small leap to great leap, more structured to more open, clearly defined problems to fuzzy problems, less independence to more independence, and slower to quicker. Each student will be at a different point along each of the continuums. For some, a single word or a photograph can be the focus. For other students, learning can be inspired by storybooks, artworks by other artists or cultures and. It all depends on the kind of stimuli your students can respond to in a meaningful way. When designing lessons for students with disabilities, the challenge is to connect what we are doing to something familiar. It could be something engaging like a photo of an animal or a wintry scene. If a student has considerable knowledge of a particular content area they may be ready for a more complex approach to the project. Or, if a student is more independent then they may require less assistance from the adults. For example, my Abstract Jungle Landscape lesson, on page 40, is foundational in terms of the ideas involved. It is abstract in the representation of the animals, simple in terms of the skills required, multi-faceted due to the number of steps involved and it allows for some independent work for the students. It is important to adjust the challenge level to meet the needs of all students.

Another component to a successful lesson plan is the involvement of some type of sensory exploration. In my experience I have found that at times it is more important to explore than to create something recognizable. For this reason, some of what is produced may be very abstract in art terms. Additionally, it may seem very abstract to the adults who are assisting in the art room, the classroom teacher or the parents. Some may question the validity of these types of lessons. Reassure those who question these abstract explorations with the fact that a lot of important brain activity is taking place as the students use their senses and motor skills. Keeping the mind engaged and stimulated through artistic endeavors encourages the growth of new brain cells, and the development of new neuropathways in the brain (Tubbs, 2008).

All lessons are aligned with one or more of the National Art Standards, which include:

1. Understanding and applying media, techniques, and processes
2. Using knowledge of structures and functions
3. Choosing and evaluating a range of subject matter, symbols, and ideas
4. Understanding the visual arts in relation to history and cultures
5. Reflecting upon and assessing the characteristics and merits of their work and the work of others
6. Making connections between visual arts and other disciplines

Once you have taken into consideration the students' abilities, how to engage the senses and how to connect with the standards, there are some other important issues to address.

First, ask yourself why you are teaching this lesson? If it does not contribute to their growth in self-expression, knowledge or skills then perhaps the lesson needs to be rethought. In some cases the lesson could connect to knowledge or skills they already have, or they are learning about in their regular classroom. Some lessons will improve motor skills, through the manipulation of materials and tools. Reading skills are aided by activities that involve differentiation and matching. Cutting, which involves tracking along a line, also improves reading. Whatever the outcome, it is critical that the experience be meaningful and expressive for the student.

Second, to make the lesson most successful, make sure you have a hook at the beginning that will engage and motivate them to participate. Students with disabilities are just like all students with regard to the importance of being engaged in learning. Using a visual hook can be enough, but engaging other senses, through the use of music for example, can be very helpful.

Once you have their attention, the third issue that is very important is preparedness. Have everything ready that you will need to complete the task. This requires step-by-step instructions and a detailed list of ingredients so the lesson can flow from beginning to end.

The fourth issue involves assessing the success of the lesson and the achievement of the students. When the lesson is over it is very important to reflect on the level of student engagement, the flow of materials and steps, the ease with which the students manipulated the materials, and the performance-based assessment of student achievement. Make notes about your reflections on the lesson for future use. Measurement of student achievement can be accomplished in a variety of ways. The next section addresses this topic.

Assessment

Structuring student assessment will be based upon your school district's grading policy and the students' IEPs. My assessment methods have changed over the years. Initially, I was assessing many skills including the student's ability to: write his/her name, draw shapes, cut on a line, use glue carefully, explore new materials, paint with a brush and water, communicate with words or other means, cooperate and clean up. Whew! It was too many criteria to evaluate in a short period of time. What was quickly discovered is that less is more when it comes to assessment. Working in an art environment is very exciting! To an outsider it may appear chaotic, but I prefer to describe it as controlled chaos. The energy and activity levels are high. Things happen fast and then it is over and time to clean up. Assessment needs to be pared down to the essential goals and must be easy to accomplish within limited time constraints, but this is not necessarily true for every group. Some students can participate in self-assessment, and the teacher's assessment can involve higher order skills. Student participation in assessment is great if you have the time and the students have the abilities. I have found that reducing my assessment to fewer criteria that align with the student's IEPs as well as the standards allows me to effectively and efficiently accomplish this important task. Here are five basic skills that are excellent goals for making assessment effective and efficient:

- Participates in art class
- Completes work
- Achieves daily goal
- Uses art materials properly and safely
- Explores new textures and materials

Having a simple, generic approach to assessment for your students places the focus of class time on creating meaningful and achievable lessons that contribute to their artistic development, as well as their view of the world and their place in it. This is more important than using some normative measurement of success or conventional views of the meaning of art.

Introduction to the Lessons

I have included in this book a large selection of lessons. Most have photos of student work. Some do not. I have tried to list all of the ingredients, but you can certainly improvise and modify to suit your situation. I have written the procedures with non-art teachers in mind, so do not be intimidated if you do not consider yourself an artist. As far as I am concerned, we are all artists. Some of us get to make art and others just have memories of making art, not all good ones unfortunately. No matter your level of expertise, you will have fun and so will your students.

Some lessons include shapes or schema that the students may not be able to draw without help. Since the goal is to encourage artistic expression, I feel that helping students to communicate through art is most important. Sometimes helping the student by placing your hand over theirs is a suitable solution; sometimes a template with a basic shape can be more appropriate. It is up to the teacher to determine when to help the student to create a recognizable shape or object and when to allow them to create a shape that is their own unique representation of the object.

My lessons are organized in four ways. The first group of lessons is focused on Making Connections to Our World, which includes a unique cityscape collage, for example. The second group of lessons is focused on Elements and Principles of Art, such as color, line, shape, texture and pattern. The third group of lessons is focused on Materials Exploration – It's About Process Not Product, which includes activities like painting on foil. And the final group, Literature, World Cultures and Artists, incorporates storybooks, the art of other countries and various artists as inspiration for art production.

Making Connections to Our World

An important emphasis for working with students with disabilities involves helping them understand the world around them. By creating art that directly connects to everyday objects, animals and places, they are gaining skills that are valuable to them as they observe and try to make sense of the world. For students on the Autism spectrum, finding order in the world is critical to peace of mind.

Cityscape

Ingredients:

- 12"x18" blue paper
- white oil pastels
- pan of black tempera paint diluted with water
- black and gray construction paper scraps or strips
- aluminum foil pieces
- scissors
- glue
- photographs of cities at night
- circular stencils

Preparation:

Prepare the diluted black paint. Cut 3-4" wide strips of black and gray paper. Cut 1" squares of aluminum foil or have foil sheets for students to cut up.

Procedure:

Show students photographs of cities at night. Discuss what they see. Demonstrate how to create a moon and stars using oil pastels. Give the students the large, blue paper, the circular stencils and the white oil pastels. After the students create their own moon and stars, demonstrate how to use the diluted black paint to brush over the blue paper, creating a night sky. Set aside to dry. Demonstrate how to cut up the wide strips of black and gray paper to make buildings. And demonstrate how to cut up the foil to make windows. Using glue, the students will arrange the buildings and attach the foil for windows on the painted paper.

This activity connects art-making with the world in which we live.

One of my students' works (pictured on the previous page) was selected for the 2010 International VSA Festival, All Kids Can Create exhibition, *State of the Art*, in Washington, DC. This artwork was chosen to represent the state of Illinois.

Volcanoes

Ingredients:

- 12"x18" sky blue paper
- 9"x12" black and gray paper
- craft scissors with a variety of blades
- glue
- pencils
- pans of diluted black, red, yellow and orange tempera paint
- brushes
- photographs of volcanoes

Preparation:

Dilute the paints. Cover the work area.

Procedure:

Observe the photographs of volcanoes and discuss them with the students. Demonstrate how to paint the diluted black paint on the sky blue paper to create a smoky atmosphere for the sky. After the students paint their sky, set the paper aside to dry. Demonstrate how to draw the shape of the volcano. Students can select gray or black paper for their volcano. After they have drawn their volcano shape, they can select a craft scissors to cut a rough edge, adding a roughness to the shape. Glue the volcano onto the smoky, blue paper. Demonstrate how to tilt the paper up and dab the red, orange or yellow paint onto the top edge of the volcano. Watch the "lava" flow down the mountain. Use all three colors using the same technique. Turn the paper around and use the colors again, tilting the paper the other direction, so the lava is spitting up into the sky.

This activity makes a wonderful connection with nature and allows gravity to add to the experience. This is a very engaging activity!

Earth Day Collage

Ingredients:

- 12"x18" lime green paper
- variety of nature stickers
- variety of nature rubber stamps and inks
- variety of animal photos
- digital photo of students (optional: use the comic book effect on Photo Booth, a Mac application)
- black and white earth template with continents outlined
- blue and green tempera paint in shallow pans
- sponges
- cartoon "bubble" that says "I love the earth!", or other message about the earth

Preparation:

Have all of the supplies ready to move through the steps. This can be done in one or two classes, allowing drying time for the painted earth.

Procedure:

Explain to the students that April 22nd is Earth Day, a special day dedicated to preserving and protecting our planet, but emphasis can be made on caring for our earth every day. Show a globe and show them where we are on the earth.   Demonstrate how to use the sponge and paints to give the land and sea some green and blue, respectively. This step may require helpers in order to keep the students from painting the whole globe randomly or with one color only. Or, they can take turns, watching their classmates paint. Set globe paintings aside to dry. Take turns using either a digital camera or the Mac application Photo Booth to create a photo of each student – if you have a globe, let them hold it for the picture! To assemble the collage, use the large green paper vertically. Cut and glue the globe and the digital photo on the green paper. Cut and glue magazine photos of animals found on land and at sea. Use the stickers and rubber stamps to decorate the poster. Display around the school to celebrate Earth Day and our students' accomplishments!

This activity allows the student to communicate about a subject in a meaningful way using art.

Butterfly & Cocoon

Ingredients:

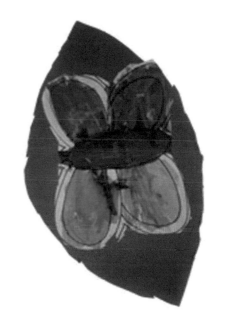

- 9"x12" tan paper
- black marker
- brown, white, black and gray coloring supplies
- white paper or template of a butterfly
- glue
- rubber bands
- scissors
- crayons
- stencils
- watercolors
- brushes
- pans for water
- photographs of butterflies, cocoons, or real ones

Preparation:

Some students may be able to draw
a butterfly shape. For those who need assistance you can create
a template of a butterfly on white paper for them to color and
paint. The book, *The Very Hungry Caterpillar*, by Eric Carle, is a
wonderful resource for this project.

Procedure:

Look at the photographs and introduce the students to cocoons and butterflies. If possible, have real cocoons and real butterflies (in frames) to pass around. Discuss the shapes, colors and patterns on the wings. Demonstrate how to draw a butterfly. You may need to use hand-over-hand assistance to help the student or use a template of a butterfly shape. Students can use stencils to create shapes on the butterfly paper or freely draw their own shapes. If a discussion of symmetry is appropriate, butterflies are a wonderful way to utilize this design principle. Otherwise, allow for a variety of shapes to be drawn all over the butterfly.

Encourage the students to apply pressure with the crayons. Some students may need hand-over-hand assistance in order to apply pressure with the crayons. Using watercolors, brush paint over the shapes and watch the wax resist the paint. The shapes magically push through the paint! For students who cannot apply sufficient pressure with the crayon, use diluted paints that will allow their shapes to show through. Set painted butterflies aside to dry.

Look at the cocoons, real or photographs, and discuss the colors, textures and lines. Using brown, white, black and gray coloring supplies draw a variety of lines all over the tan paper. Draw a large football shape that fills the paper using the black marker.

Cut out the shape. When rolled, this will be the cocoon. Once the butterfly is dry, cut it out and glue it on the back of the cocoon (the blank side of the tan paper). Roll and rubber band to keep it closed like a cocoon.

This activity uses observed nature for the subject in art.

Abstract American Flag

Ingredients:

- 12"x18" white paper
- 6"x6" cardboard
- masking tape
- newspaper
- dish liquid or liquid soap
- red tempera and blue tempera mixed with liquid soap in separate pans
- bubble wand or bent pipe cleaner for wand
- red and blue large crayons
- red and blue star stickers
- star-shaped rubber stamps
- red and blue ink pads

Preparation:

Cover the table with newspaper. Mix equal parts of paint and dish liquid in a pan. Tape a piece of cardboard over the upper left-hand corner of the white paper to save space for the stars on the flag.

Procedure:

Discuss and examine the American flag, the shapes, the stripes, and the colors. Demonstrate how to use the crayons to draw stripes on the flag. Drawing lines with the crayons may require some assistance. Also, feel free to use both red and blue for the stripes as this will not be a realistic flag. With assistance, students blow red and blue bubbles onto the paper, creating red and blue circles when they pop. The popping is the best part! This step is best done as a station for one student at a time. Remove the cardboard and use the star stickers, star rubber stamps and ink to fill the corner with various stars.

This activity allows the student to create a recognizable object in an abstract manner.

Abstract Jungle Landscape

Ingredients:

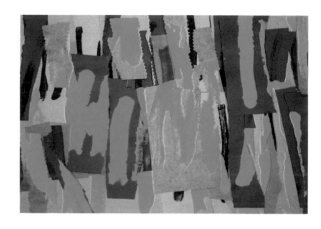

- 12"x18" lime green paper
- 6"x9" white, orange, light gray, dark green and marbled papers
- brushes
- glue
- black, dark gray and light green tempera paint
- photos of jungle animals, stuffed jungle animals or Henri Rousseau's jungle landscapes

Procedure:

Show the students photos of jungle animals, paintings of jungles, or stuffed jungle animals. Talk about patterns on the plants and animals. Demonstrate how to make stripes using a brush and paint. Using the paints, students will create the black striped pattern of the tiger on orange paper and the zebra on white paper, as well as the wrinkled gray lines of an elephant. They will also make tall grasses with lime green lines on dark green paper and marbled paper. When dry, demonstrate how to tear strips of paper for the animals so they appear to be running through the jungle. Using the large, lime green papers horizontally, glue the animal-patterned strips onto the green background. Finally, tear strips of the dark green and marbled "grasses" and glue them on top of the animals, keeping everything in a vertical direction. Not everyone will glue everything vertically. That's OK. The animals will be hiding in the jungle anyway.

This activity allows the child to create a meaningful landscape in an abstract manner.

Animal Noses

Ingredients:

- 3 oz. paper cups (not plastic)
- tempera paint in pans
- large paint brushes
- animal photos
- hole punch
- thin yarn
- markers

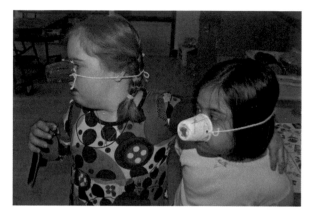

Important to note: This activity is intended for young children only. In order to preserve the dignity of students with disabilities it is always important to consider the age appropriateness of an activity.

Preparation:

If the cups are patterned or colorful, you will need to paint them white and allow them to dry.

Procedure:

Look at and discuss animal pictures. Ask them what animal they would like to be. Animal Beanie Babies, animal masks or plastic animal noses can also be a resource. Demonstrate how to brush the appropriate colored paint on the outside of the cup, such as brown for a monkey. Ask the student what color paint they will need for their animal nose. Students then paint their cups the colors of their animals' noses. This is quite quick, and they have to dry before moving on. Set this project aside and do something else such as drawing pictures of the animals. When dry, discuss the animals again, noting patterns, fur, nostrils, and any other distinguishing features on the nose of the animal. Give students markers to add the patterns and details to complete their noses. Punch holes and string to fit with yarn. Tie behind the head, loosely. Have fun being animals!

This activity connects art-making with nature, dramatic play and imagination.

Themed Books

Themed books can be a fun way to explore a shape related to academic learning. The following example uses butterflies as the theme, but any subject with a simple shape would work well.

Ingredients:

- white cardstock blank or printed with the outline of a large butterfly (4/student)
- crayons (glitter crayons are fun)
- shape stencils
- diluted glitter paint in pans
- large brushes
- scissors
- brass fasteners
- hole punch

Procedure:

Introduce the concept of butterflies. Look at books or posters about butterflies. Discuss the shapes, patterns and symmetry on the wings. Demonstrate how to create shapes and patterns on the butterfly pages using stencils or allow random designs. Give each student four pieces of white cardstock with butterflies outlined (or blank cardstock for students to draw their own butterfly shapes) and crayons. Help them draw patterns and shapes all over the butterflies. Once the butterflies are decorated with patterns and shapes, pass around pans of diluted glitter paint to brush over their patterns. When dry, cut out the butterflies and punch a hole in the upper left-hand corner of each page. Assemble using the brass fasteners.

Variation:

Students could use a computer to create typed sentences with facts about butterflies to cut and glue on each page of their books.

This activity connects the art of bookmaking with observed nature.

Chalk Flower

Ingredients:

- 12"x18" lime green and orange paper
- warm colored chalk (red, yellow, orange, pink)
- cool colored chalk (blue, green, purple)
- diluted white tempera in pans
- large brushes
- scissors
- glue
- 6" circle stencil
- real flowers and/or photographs of flowers

Procedure:

Look at flowers and discuss the parts and shapes. Demonstrate how to fill the orange paper with warm-colored chalk lines using the tip of the chalk, not the side. Use the same technique with the green paper and cool-colored chalk lines. Demonstrate how to brush on the diluted white tempera over the chalk. Use a separate pan of diluted white paint for warm and cool colors. They will enjoy seeing and feeling how the chalk blends under the brush. When dry, assist students in tracing and cutting: a 6"circle, 18" long stem, and a 6" long leaf on the green paper.

For the petals, you can trace and cut 7 or 8 elongated football shapes. Cut them in half to have plenty of petals. Flip over the circle and work on the back. Flip over the petals and glue them around the edge of the back of the circle. Consequently, the front of the circle and the petals will have the painted surface. If you run a thin line of glue around the back edge of the circle it will be easier to place the petals around it. Glue on the stem to the back of the circle. Glue on the leaf to the stem to finish. Allow to dry.

This activity uses observed nature for the subject in art and includes an enjoyable sensory experience with the paint and chalk.

Holiday House Collage

Ingredients:

- 12"x18" white paper
- house stencil
- sponges
- glitter or sequins
- fake snow
- glue
- masking tape
- trays or boxes for glitter and fake snow
- pans of primary-colored tempera paint

Preparation:

Cut the paper to fit the stencil. A washable stencil can be rinsed between students. If using tag board stencils, you will need one for each student. Tape the stencil over the paper onto a hard work surface, or hold the stencil in place over the paper.

Procedure:

Discuss how houses look during the holidays: decorative lights, snow, etc. Let the students feel the textures of the sponges, glitter, and snow and discuss texture. Ask them to feel their hair, clothing, and table to deepen their understanding of texture. Allow each student to pick two primary colors, using one sponge for each. Guide them to fill the house with sponge prints. Notice how the primary colors mix to create secondary colors. Dribble glue onto the roof, or wherever decorative lights are desired. Sprinkle glitter or sequins onto glue. Dribble glue on or around house and sprinkle fake snow onto glue.

This activity allows the student to create a work of art based upon personal observations and experiences.

Themed Collage

Themed collages can be a fun way of exploring a shape related to academic learning and/or the world around us. The following example uses leaves for the theme.

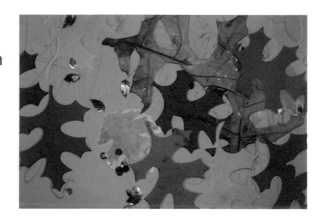

Ingredients:
- white paper or a color of paper related to the theme/subject (could be a large leaf shape or green paper for grass in this example)
- coloring supplies, autumn colors work well
- leaf-shaped supplies, such as stickers, tissue or silk leaves, leaf stencils, leaf-shaped sponges, leaf-shaped rubber stamps and ink pads
- tempera paint and/or glitter paint in pans
- real leaves for printmaking
- printing ink and ink brayer (roller)
- glue
- scissors

Procedure:

Introduce the concept of the leaf shape. Take a walk and look for leaf shapes outside. Demonstrate how to create a leaf shape using a stencil. Give each student a large piece of paper, and leaf-shaped stencil. Help them to draw leaves all over the paper. Pass around various materials that are leaf-shaped. The shapes can be pre-cut or the students can cut their own pieces. Glue the leaf-shaped items on the paper. Finish the collage using leaf-shaped sponges dipped in tempera or glitter paint, or use real leaves rolled with ink to print leaf shapes on the paper.

This activity connects academic content matter with art-making.

Bird Sculptures

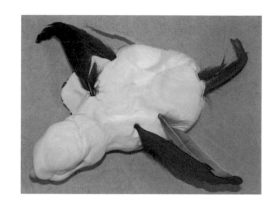

Ingredients:

- colored modeling compound
- large beads
- colorful feathers

Procedure:

Discuss and look at birds or pictures of birds. Note parts such as head, eyes, beak, body, legs, wings and tail. Give each student a choice of colored modeling compound. Mixing more than one color together is fun! Demonstrate how to squish, push, and pinch the material to create a body and head. Students can play with the material, enjoying the sensory experience before forming their birds. Students can add feathers for wings and a tail. Students can add beads or other supplies to give their bird eyes and beaks, or to simply make them "fancy" or "fanciful". Allow to dry. Variation: Once dry, students can draw on the birds with marker or paint them.

Working with the modeling compound to create a three-dimensional creature builds a connection between art-making and nature.

Polar Landscape

Ingredients:

- 12"x18" sky blue paper
- 6"x12" white paper
- white scraps of paper
- very light gray tempera paint
- sponges
- glue
- craft scissors with a variety of blades
- white paper for drawing polar animals, such as a seal, polar bear, penguin, or walrus
- crayons
- rubber stamp animal tracks and ink pads
- photos of polar landscapes and animals

Preparation:

Some of your students may have difficulty drawing polar animals. You can help them using the hand-over-hand approach. You can also prepare some small templates of the polar animals and have them ready for the students to use. Have the crayons needed to color the animals so you do not end up with purple penguins. (We are trying to connect with our world, after all!)

Procedure:

Show the students photos of polar landscapes and animals. Ask them what they see. Discuss the animals and the snowy, icy land. Demonstrate how to cut across the middle of the 6"x12" white paper to create two pieces, each 12" in length with a varied edge, like mountains. Demonstrate how to glue one piece at the very bottom of the vertically-positioned sky blue paper, for the land. Leave a space for the ocean and glue the other half of the white paper near the top for mountains, leaving space above for sky. Make icebergs using the craft scissors and small pieces of white scraps. Glue the icebergs in the ocean section of the picture. Color, cut and glue the polar animals on the land and/or icebergs. Use the rubber stamps to create tracks for the animals. Finish with sponge painting using very light gray tempera for falling snow.

This project can best be accomplished in two days. The first day the students can cut and glue the white papers and the animals, after coloring them. The second day they can use the rubber stamps for animal tracks and add the sponge painted snow. Otherwise it can get quite sloppy!

This activity facilitates an understanding of how to create a meaningful landscape using a variety of materials.

Desert Landscape

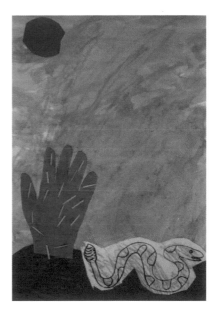

Ingredients:

- 12"x18" white paper
- 6"x12" sandpaper (or tan paper painted with a mixture of sand and brown paint)
- 3" squares of orange, red, and yellow paper
- various green papers, 6"x9"
- toothpicks
- white paper for making a snake
- diluted orange and red tempera paint in pans
- brushes
- glue
- pencils
- scissors
- circle stencil
- photographs of desert scenes, plants, animals, and sunsets

Preparation:

Some of your students may have difficulty making a snake. You can help them with the hand-over-hand approach or you can create a template of snakes or desert animals and have them ready. For the sand, if you are using tan paper and paint mixed

with sand, prepare the paint mixture. Cut toothpicks into ½"
pieces for the students to use as cactus needles.

Procedure:

Show photographs of desert scenes, plants, animals and
sunsets. Discuss what the students see. Position the white
paper vertically and demonstrate how to use the diluted orange
and red tempera paints to create a sunset-colored sky. Set
aside to dry. Demonstrate how to paint the tan paper with the
sandy brown paint, and leave to dry. Or, if using sandpaper,
position it horizontally and demonstrate how to cut the paper to
create sandy hills and set aside. With adult assistance, trace the
students' hand on any color green paper with a pencil. Trace
over the pencil with a black marker, so the students can cut out
the "cactus". It is a tricky shape to cut, so assistance may be
needed. Give the students the broken toothpick pieces to glue
onto the cactus. Set aside to dry. Color and cut the snakes or
other desert animals. Allow students to select red, yellow, or
orange paper to use for their sun. Demonstrate how to trace
and cut out a circle for the sun and set aside. Once everything
is dry, glue the sand, sun and animals on the sunset-painted
paper

This activity facilitates an understanding of how to create a
meaningful landscape using a variety of materials.

Elements and Principles of Art

The elements and principles of art are the basic building blocks with which art is made. The elements of art are: line, value, shape, form, space, color and texture. The principles of art are: balance, contrast, movement, emphasis, pattern, proportion and unity. (See the Glossary at the end of this text for further explanation) These basic components of art are critical to the students' self-expression and successful communication of ideas. In order for the student to create meaningful art and make connections to the world in which they live they need to work with the elements and principles of art throughout the year. These lessons can be revisited using different materials each year as a means to reinforce learning.

Altered Books: Colors

Ingredients:

- hardcover, used books
- variety of collage materials
- scissors
- glue
- chipboard or poster board
- glitter paint
- pans
- brushes
- low temperature glue gun

Preparation:

Remove any covers or stickers from the books that will prevent the students from attaching their collage materials. Decide on a theme for the books (I used colors) and collect the necessary collage materials.

Procedure:

For making the color books the students paint two facing pages with one color of glitter paint. This is a transparent paint, so the illustrations/words show through, adding to the collage. While the paint dries students can do a related activity with the selected color, such as pumpkin paintings for the color orange. Once the book pages are dry the students cut, arrange and glue a variety of materials of the same color and create their monochromatic collages. Some three-dimensional objects require the teacher to use a low-temperature glue gun to attach the items to the page. When the two page collage is done, a piece of chipboard, cut to size, can be glued between the finished page and the next page for support. The following week the process is repeated until all of the pages are finished.

Once the book pages are complete a cover design can be created. The book will not close completely due to the collage materials. A ribbon can be attached around the book and tied to keep the book together, if desired.

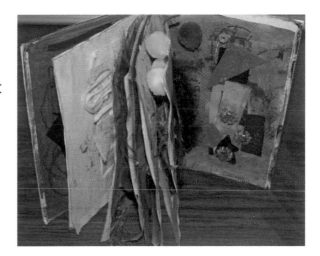

This activity focuses on color while providing an opportunity for self-expression with a variety of materials.

Color Wheel

Ingredients:

- white construction paper
- paper cups
- paint brushes
- red, yellow and blue tempera paint
- color wheel

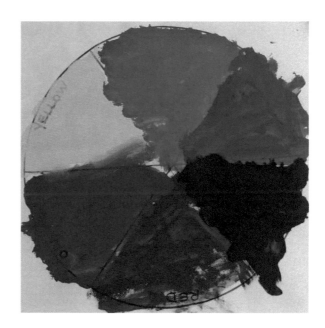

Preparation:

If your students can write the color words then you would only need a white paper and a circle stencil. If needed, prepare the white paper by drawing a large circle to fill the page. Divide the circle into six sections and label them with the colors on the wheel, in the correct order: yellow, orange, red, purple (or violet), blue and green. Prepare one paper for each student. Pour a small amount of red paint into a paper cup for each student, as well a cup of yellow and a cup of blue.

Procedure:

This lesson will be exciting because of the paint, so if possible have help. Introduce the students to the color wheel and have them identify the colors. Demonstrate how to paint one "pie piece" with yellow, for example, then add a small amount of red to the yellow to create orange for the next "pie piece". Depending upon the amount of help you have available, it may be necessary to work with one child at a time while the others watch. It is fun to mix the primary colors to create the secondary colors. It is important to supervise the painting; otherwise the entire wheel will be painted with one color before you turn around! After yellow and orange, use red in the next section. Add blue to the red to create purple for the next section. Use blue for the next section. Finish by adding yellow to the blue to make green for the final section. For some students it helps to outline the section with the corresponding color of paint and they can easily fill in the section.

Developing an understanding of the color wheel and mixing colors is an important skill for any artist.

Line Painting

Ingredients:

- colored paper
- contrasting colored paint in a pan
- thick string, rope, or yarn

Procedure:

Introduce the concept of line. Look for lines in the room or on the children's clothing. Demonstrate how to create a line by dipping a thick string in paint and placing it on a piece of paper. Give each student a large piece of paper. Have them dip the yarn and place it on the paper. Repeat the process several times, dipping the string in the paint and placing it on the paper. This activity may require the assistance of an adult's hand over the child's hand. Or, one student can work with the string while the others watch. When finished, look at the paintings and discuss what can be seen in the shapes created by the random line placement. They might identify simple shapes or see familiar objects, such as a whale in this example.

This is a wonderful opportunity to use imagination to find meaning in something that has been randomly created.

Shape Collage

Ingredients:

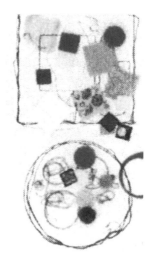

- white paper
- coloring supplies
- round and square objects, papers and images such as pizza
- round and square stencils
- tempera paint and/or glitter paint in pans
- round cups, square boxes
- round and square sponges
- scrap paper
- scissors
- glue

Procedure:

Introduce the concept of shape. Look for shapes in the room or on the children's clothing. Demonstrate how to create a shape using a stencil. Give each student a large piece of white paper and have them create a large square and a large circle next to each other. Give them time to draw smaller squares and circles inside of the larger ones, using stencils and a variety of coloring supplies. Pass around various materials that are circular and square-shaped or the students can cut their own pieces from scraps. Glue the circular and square-shaped items into their respective matching shapes. Finish the shape collage using circular and square-shaped sponges, cups, and boxes dipped in tempera or glitter paint.

Variation:

Use triangles and octagons or other pairs of shapes.

This lesson provides an opportunity to create patterns and rhythm through repetition of shapes.

Color Collage

Choose a color to focus on and give parents advance knowledge so the students can wear that color to school on that day. Collect as many art materials as possible of the selected color for the students to explore, arrange, color, cut, and glue.

Ingredients:
- large white paper
- tempera paint in pans
- patterned foam paint rollers
- stickers
- coloring supplies
- stencils
- colored masking tape
- fabric scraps
- feathers, buttons, and other miscellaneous materials
- patterned papers or gift wrap
- scissors
- glue
- colored glitter
- rubber stamps and ink pads
- Playdoh in selected color (or two primary colors that can be mixed to produce the secondary color of the day)

Procedure:

Introduce the color of choice and look for it in the room or on the students' clothing. Pass out the paper and coloring supplies. Invite them to color anything that they want using the color of the day. Some students will color briefly, while others will spend more time coloring. Some may use stencils, while others may draw freehand. As each student finishes the coloring step pass out baskets of supplies. Invite each student to select, explore, arrange, color, cut and glue. When each student completes their collage give them one or more of the "finishing touches": rubber stamps with ink pads, tempera paint with paint rollers, and/or glitter. As an extra activity, pass around colored Playdoh to manipulate. If working with a secondary color (orange, green and purple) give the students the two primary colors of Playdoh to combine and make the secondary color.

Variations:

Some colors may suggest commonplace objects, such as pumpkins for orange. Students could work on a large pumpkin-shaped piece of white paper to fill with orange materials. Or, you could use only metallic materials; or, use color groups or pairs, such as red, white, and blue. Or, create a book of color collages – see Altered Books lesson on page 58.

Using various materials of a single color is a wonderful way to develop an understanding of texture and variety.

Black & White Collage

Ingredients:

- black and white paper
- black and white coloring supplies
- black and white patterned papers and materials
- glue
- scissors

Preparation:

Cut a 12"x18" piece of black paper to 6"x18" and glue it onto the 12"x18" white paper.

Procedure:

Introduce the principle of contrast. Look for black and white things in the room to demonstrate the meaning of contrast. Give each student a large piece of ½ black and ½ white papers and have them use black coloring supplies on the white side and white coloring supplies on the black side. Pass around the black and white collage supplies. The students can cut out their own pieces of white and black papers and/or use some pre-cut supplies. Glue the black and white materials onto the opposite colored half of the paper.

Variation:

This project can be done using any pair of contrasting colors such as complementary colors (blue/orange, red/green, yellow/purple), adding paint using patterned rollers, and/or using rubber stamps and ink pads. The more varied the materials the more interesting the experience and results.

This is a wonderful activity for developing an understanding of the principle of contrast.

Contour Line Drawing

Contour lines follow around the shape of an object. Students enjoy tracing around the shape of commonplace objects, such as school supplies.

Ingredients:

- pencils
- erasers
- large white paper
- various school supplies such as glue bottles, paint sets and scissors

Procedure:

Introduce the concept of contour line by drawing around the edge of a commonplace object such as a glue bottle. Demonstrate how to lay the object on the paper and hold the pencil upright, as you trace around the object. Emphasize keeping the pencil straight for best results. Distribute paper and pencils and invite students to select an object to begin their drawing. Some assistance may be required to keep pencils on a straight path. Once the objects have been traced, the details found on the objects can be drawn, such as labels or product names, like Elmer's Glue.

Variation:

Trace around the objects with crayon and brush watercolors over the objects, creating a wax resist painting.

This activity facilitates an understanding of the distinction between geometric and non-geometric shapes.

Pattern Collage

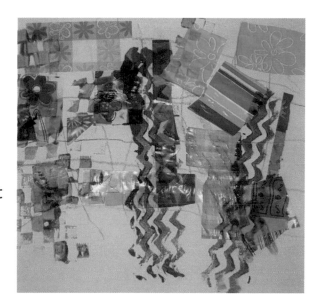

Ingredients:

- white paper
- coloring supplies
- patterned gift wrap
- foamy, patterned paint rollers
- glitter paint
- glue
- scissors

Procedure:

Introduce the principle of pattern. Look for patterns in the room or on the children's clothing. Demonstrate how to create a line pattern using a crayon. Give each student a large piece of white paper and have them create line patterns all over it. Pass around patterned gift wrap. Students can cut their own pieces of the gift wrap or they can use pre-cut pieces. Glue patterned gift wrap onto the paper. Finish the patterned collage using foamy, patterned paint rollers with glitter paint. Any water-based paint will work. This last step may require the assistance of an adult's hand over the child's hand.

This collage activity develops an understanding of pattern and variety.

Line Collage

Collect as many art materials as possible for the students to explore, arrange, color, cut, and glue.

Ingredients:
- large white paper
- coloring supplies
- thin paint brushes
- tempera paint in pans
- string
- yarn
- pipe cleaners
- ribbon
- line-patterned, foam paint roller
- scissors
- glue

Procedure:

Introduce the concept of lines and look for lines in the room and on the students' clothing. Demonstrate ways to make lines using coloring supplies and thin brushes dipped in paint. Pass out the paper and coloring supplies. Invite them to color lines all over their paper. Some students will color briefly, while others will spend more time coloring. As each student finishes the coloring step, pass out baskets of supplies and invite each student to select, explore, arrange, color, cut and glue. When finished, students can roll paint lines over their collage with the foam paint rollers.

This activity develops an understanding of the element of line and the concept of variety.

Shapes and Colors Collage

Ingredients:

- wax paper
- colored tissue pieces
- glue and water solution in pans
- thick paint brushes
- mats for framing
- masking tape
- scissors
- photographs of stained glass or real stained glass artwork

Preparation:

Dilute glue with water so it can be brushed over the tissue.

Procedure:

Discuss the concept of stained glass windows while viewing pictures or a real example. Demonstrate how to brush the glue and water mixture over pieces of tissue onto a large piece of wax paper. Allow each student to choose a variety of pieces of colored tissue paper to cut, arrange and glue on a piece of wax paper. Brushing on the glue and water mixture may require the assistance of an adult's hand over the child's hand. Finish the tissue collage by "framing" it with a pre-cut mat. You can use masking tape on the back to attach the wax paper to the frame.

Variation:

Once the glue is dry, coloring supplies could be used to add shapes or patterns on the tissue paper. Another approach can include a frame made of clay. See Clay "Stained Glass" Window on the next page.

This activity facilitates an understanding of how colors and shapes can change when they are overlapped.

Clay "Stained Glass" Window

Ingredients:

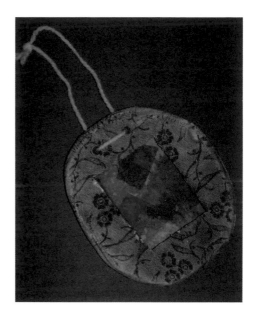

- wax paper
- colored tissue pieces
- glue and water solution in pans
- thick paint brushes
- clay for framing
- brown tempera
- sponges
- water
- kiln
- yarn
- plastic knife
- 1/4" diameter stick or pencil
- rolling pin
- burlap
- lace
- 3"x3" piece of cardboard

Procedure:

See the Shapes and Colors Collage lesson, on the previous page, for making the wax paper and tissue "stained glass" and make it 4"x4". Set aside the wax and tissue collage to dry.

Demonstrate how to roll out clay to create an oval-shaped slab.

Use the 3"x3" piece of cardboard and a plastic knife to cut out a window in the slab. Or, use a sturdy plastic cup to press into the clay, making a round window. Use a stick or pencil to poke two holes through the clay, side-by-side, at one end of the slab (see photograph of student work). These holes will be used for a loop of yarn to hang up the finished piece. Lay a piece of lace over the clay slab and roll over it, leaving a lacy texture in the clay. Allow to dry and fire in kiln. After bisque fire, brush brown tempera paint over the textured side, then gently wash it off, leaving a stain in the lacy texture. When dry, finish by gluing the small wax paper "stained glass" window on the back of the clay opening and string up the yarn though the holes. Hang it in the window to catch the sun.

This activity facilitates an understanding of texture, as well as how colors and shapes can change when they are overlapped.

Texture Books

Bookmaking can be a fun way of exploring any subject. The following example is about texture.

Ingredients:
- 6"x9" white cardstock
- primary and secondary-colored tempera and glitter paints in pans
- additives for paints, such as sand, wax flakes, fake snow and gloss medium
- big brushes
- scissors
- pencils
- stapler
- typed texture words (rough and smooth)

Preparation:
Mix additives with paints to create some rough and some smooth textured paints. Print out texture words for students to cut and attach to the pages of the book.

Procedure:
Introduce the concept of texture by instructing the students to feel the table, their hair, their clothing and other textures they can find in the room. Focus on rough and smooth, or another

pair of textures. Each student spreads each of the textured paints over separate pieces of cardstock. Give students paper and pencil to write the texture words or use paper with typed texture words. Let them feel the pages and help them determine which word goes with each texture and glue the appropriate word to the corresponding textured page. Using a smooth page for the cover, help the students trace around their hand on the smooth page and write TEXTURE inside the hand shape or cut out the typed word. Assemble the book using a stapler or string together using holes punched in the pages and yarn. Read, feel and enjoy.

This activity facilitates an understanding of the element of texture and introduces bookmaking as an art form.

Materials Exploration: It's About Process Not Product

Sensory exploration is a very important part of learning for students with disabilities. At the elementary level it is a great way to engage the students in art activities. The results may appear very abstract to the untrained observer, but a closer examination will reveal some wonderful textures, layers, patterns and shapes. There are many surprises to be found and celebrated in these explorations. These activities provide students with a pleasurable way to express their feelings and develop a personal aesthetic.

Foil Painting

Ingredients:

- aluminum foil
- cardboard
- tempera paint in pans (warm and cool colors)
- large brushes
- glitter
- glue
- masking tape

Preparation:

Wrap a large piece of aluminum foil over a piece of heavy cardboard for each student and tape it on the back.

Procedure:

Introduce the concept of shiny and dull. Look for shiny and dull things in the room. Demonstrate how to paint over the foil, creating dull spots, leaving shiny foil areas. Notice how the brush glides over the foil providing a very pleasing, sensory experience that is different from painting on paper. Drizzle glue on the painting and sprinkle glitter and/or attach sequins.

This activity develops an understanding of texture and color.

Layered Painting

Ingredients:

- 12"x18" tan paper
- variety of shape stencils
- variety of crayons
- diluted white tempera paint in pans
- glitter paint in pans
- large brushes

Procedure:

Discuss shapes with students. Look for shapes around the room and on the students' clothing. Demonstrate how to trace shapes all over the paper using the crayons and the stencils. Students select stencils and crayons and trace shapes onto their papers. Students brush diluted white tempera paint over areas of their drawing. Students brush glitter paint over areas of their drawing. Allow to dry. Enjoy the lovely, harmonious layers of color over the shapes.

This activity develops an understanding of shape, color, texture and unity.

Monoprints

Ingredients:

- 9"x12" light-colored paper
- printing brayers
- pans or cookie sheets
- masking tape
- 8"x10" framing mats
- black, water-based printing ink
- variety of small pieces of objects and textured materials such as: burlap, lace, ribbon, puzzle pieces, foil, fabrics, netting, bubble wrap, etc.

Preparation:

Review the section entitled Thoughts on Printmaking, on page 18. Precut a variety of textures. Attach a framing mat directly to the table (no table covers or newspaper!) in front of each child's seat, using the masking tape to create a hinge effect along one edge of the mat. This will allow the students to lift up the frame to roll out the ink on the table before closing the frame and designing the print. Monoprint means one print. Unlike typical printing in which you create a block of some type and make multiple copies of the same image.

Procedure:

Demonstrate the process. It is fascinating. First, flip the mat on its hinge, as if turning the page of a book. In the place where the mat will flip back, roll out black ink directly on the table, in an approximate rectangle.

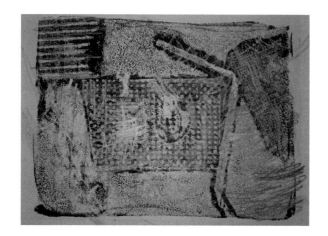

The snapping sound created by rolling out the ink is very engaging, as is the act of rolling the brayer. Flip the mat back, possibly covering some of the edges of the ink. Press a variety of textures directly on the ink, arranging them in an interesting way. Carefully place the paper on top of the textures and hold the paper still with one hand, while gently rubbing over the entire paper with the other hand. You will feel the textures through the paper. After rubbing for a couple of minutes lift the paper and reveal the print. The shapes of the textured objects will be visible against the black ink background. Set the print aside to dry.

Gently remove the textured objects and discard them. The ink on the table is still wet enough for a second, yet different print. Place a clean piece of paper over the area once again. Hold the paper still with one hand, but this time as you rub with the other hand you will not feel any textures. When the print is lifted the textured objects will show up on the paper, with a grayer look. This process will require helpers and/or perhaps the students will take turns, watching while they wait. It is a very engaging process. It is very important to hold the paper still and rub. Once the prints are dry it is fun to add color using colored pencils or oil pastels.

This activity facilitates an understanding of texture and shape. It is also interesting to compare the two prints and find similarities and differences.

Marble Painting

Ingredients:

- 10"x16" colored construction paper
- tempera paints in pans
- marbles
- large oatmeal container or similar, lidded cylinder.
- spoons

Procedure:

Roll and place a piece of paper inside of the oatmeal canister. Place a marble in the paint pan and spoon it into the container. Cover the container with the lid. Demonstrate how to press your hands against both the cover and bottom of the canister and shake it around, listening to the marble bouncing around inside. Music and dancing are fun to include with this step. Give each student a turn using the oatmeal container and as many colors as desired. When the student's turn is over, remove the painting to dry.

This activity allows the student to use their imagination to find something meaningful in the random lines created by the rolling marble.

Glittery Name Painting

Ingredients:

- 12"x18" colored paper
- tempera paint in pans
- large crayons
- glitter
- box that is larger than the paper

Procedure:

Demonstrate how to write your name using huge letters on the paper with a crayon. Demonstrate how to dip your finger in paint and trace over the crayon letters. Emphasize repeated dipping for best results. When finished tracing over the name with paint place the paper in the box and allow the student to sprinkle glitter on the painted letters. Sand can be sprinkled for a fun texture! Allow to dry. Some names may be more recognizable than others.

This activity provides a pleasurable sensory experience for the students as they create something recognizable and personal.

Salt Painting

Ingredients:

- salt
- watercolors
- large paint brushes
- pans of water
- large, white, heavy, construction paper or watercolor paper

Procedure:

Introduce how to use watercolors, dipping the brush into the water between color changes. Varied degrees of success in brush cleaning will result in many beautiful colors or many beautiful browns! Give each student a large piece of white construction paper and give them the freedom to enjoy brushing various colors all over it. When finished (this may require you to stop them at some point, before the whole thing gets muddy or torn from too much moisture) give each student a small cup of salt to sprinkle over the painting. Watch the paints change then brush off the salt. Notice the interesting texture created by the salt in the paint.

This activity is a wonderful exploration of color and texture.

Positive/Negative Space

Ingredients:

- 12"x18" white paper
- colored pencils or crayons
- masking tape

Procedure:

Demonstrate how to tear and apply long pieces of tape onto the white paper. Make sure to smooth the tape out flat.

Demonstrate how to use a variety of colors and coloring supplies to color over the tape, layering colors, scribbling, etc. When the paper is filled with color, carefully remove all of the tape! It's magic.

This activity provides the student with an opportunity to explore positive and negative space and as well as the illusion of depth.

Wet on Wet Exploration

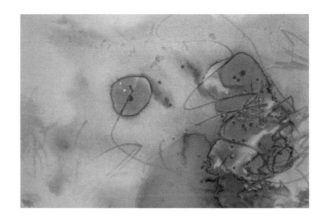

Ingredients:
- watercolor paper
- water-based markers

Preparation:

Have a sink available or a

large pan of water and lots of paper towels!

Procedure:

Demonstrate how to dip the paper into the water, making it quite saturated with water. Draw over the wet paper with water-based markers creating lines, shapes and dots. If the marker stays in one spot for an extended time it creates a wonderful blob of color. This is a project that is so engaging the students will want to do over and over again!

This engaging activity provides an opportunity to explore color, line and shape.

Yarn and Oil Pastel Line Exploration

Ingredients:

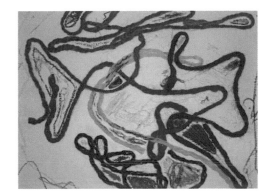

- glue and water mixture in pans
- scissors
- oil pastels
- various colors of thick yarn
- heavy weight, white cardboard

Preparation:

Cut a variety of lengths of various colors of thick yarn.

Procedure:

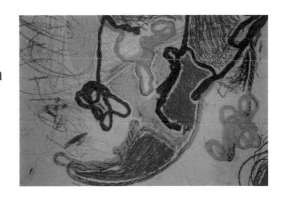

Demonstrate how to dip the yarn in the glue and water mixture, and spread the yarn out flat on the cardboard. The yarn can be repositioned to create interesting shapes. Leave the board to dry. Once the board is completely dry, the students will find that the texture of the yarn has changed from soft to hard. Next, demonstrate how to apply layers of light and dark-colored oil pastel to fill in the shapes, as well as the rest of the white cardboard.

This is an engaging exploration of texture and color mixing.

Painting Without a Brush!

Ingredients:

- 9"x12" primary-colored paper
- secondary-colored tempera paints
- pans
- glue
- pencils
- 12"x18" bright-colored paper
- craft scissors with a variety of blades
- a variety of "tools" to apply paint, such as: plastic bags, feathers, cotton swabs, netting, edge of corrugated cardboard, toothbrushes, sponges, sponge rollers, forks, string, yarn, etc.

Preparation:

Have all of your tools ready and a variety of colors of paint in pans.

Procedure:

Demonstrate how to use the various tools to create patterns and textures all over the paper. (Optional approach includes matching up complementary colored paper and paint: orange with blue, green with red, purple with yellow.)

Allow painted papers to dry. To prepare for the next class, cut the 9"x12" painted papers into 1"x12" strips for the students to cut into smaller pieces, using craft scissors. To finish, glue the small pieces all over the 12"x18", brightly-colored paper.

Variation:

The 1"x12" strips of painted paper can be woven through a larger piece of paper that has been sliced at one inch intervals in the middle. Keep the ends of the larger paper intact and weave the strips through the sliced area.

This activity is a wonderful exploration of color and contrast.

Gluey Gooey Line Printing

Ingredients:

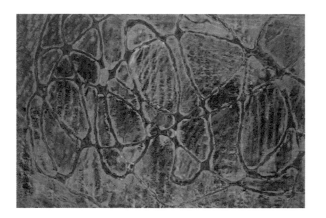

- glue bottles
- black water-based ink
- printing brayer
- pans or cookie sheets
- oil pastels
- 10"x16" corrugated cardboard
- 12"x18" white paper

Procedure:

Review the section entitled Thoughts on Printmaking, on page 18. Demonstrate how to apply thick glue lines using a glue bottle. This step may require hand-over-hand guidance by an adult. Allow to dry. Next class, roll out black water-based ink onto a pan or cookie sheet and roll the ink onto the entire board. There will be areas that do not take ink because of the height difference created by the glue. That's OK. Once the entire area is wet with ink, place the white paper on top and hold it still with one hand. Rub the back of the white paper with the other hand. It is important to keep the paper still while rubbing in order to get a good print. Add fresh ink and make as many prints as desired on any color paper. Allow prints to dry. Choose one print to add oil pastel on top of the dried ink. Layer the colors.

Try light colors on top of darker ones. (Another option is to apply color to the dry print using any coloring supplies or watercolors. Warning: the watercolors reactivate the ink and things can get rather smeary, so keep the water under control.)

This activity is a wonderful exploration of texture and color.

Literature, World Cultures, and Artists

In alignment with the national art standard focused on understanding the visual arts in relation to history and cultures, the following lessons incorporate literature, world cultures, and artists as inspiration for making art. Some students may be able to participate in art appreciation discussions which can include searching for colors and shapes, or talking about what is going on in the picture.

Whimsical Mobile

Ingredients:

- 12" brightly-colored paper squares
- 2" colored paper circles
- colored straws (larger variety) pre-cut into one inch lengths
- thin yarn, knotted at one end, wrapped in masking tape at the other end
- hole punch
- pencil
- scissors

Procedure:

Introduce the concept of sculpture and three-dimensionality. Look for sculpture or 3D objects in the room. Share the sculptural art of Alexander Calder. Demonstrate how to punch holes in the center of the paper circles. The pressure required for punching holes may require assistance. Demonstrate how to string paper circles and straw pieces over the taped end of the yarn. Students choose a piece of yarn and string up straws and circles. Demonstrate how to draw a large spiral on the large paper and how to cut on the spiral pencil line. Students select a large piece of colored paper, draw a spiral, cut along the spiral line and punch a hole at one end. Tie the spiral onto the end of the yarn. Hang up and enjoy!

This activity develops an understanding of form and provides an opportunity to see how three-dimensional art interacts with the world around it, as it twists and turns.

Glittery Numbers

Ingredients:

- 12"x18" white paper
- glitter paint, various colors
- pans for paint
- number-shaped sponges **or** sponges and number-shaped stencils
- Jasper Johns' series of numbers prints

Procedure:

Show the art of Jasper Johns, specifically his series of prints filled with numbers. Discuss what the students see. Demonstrate how to use the number-shaped sponges (or the number-shaped stencils and sponges) with the glitter paint. Dip and press the numbers all over the paper, in various directions. Use a variety of numbers and colors of paint. Pair up sponges with particular paint colors to avoid mixing the colors and making everything brown! This lesson will require helping hands or the students can take turns to keep things under control. Without proper supervision, the sponges can be overused and the paper can become covered with unrecognizable blobs! Also, when using sponges two tips are important to note. First, use a shallow layer of paint in the pans. Second, moisten the sponges with clean water before dipping them in the paint.

This engaging activity provides an opportunity for students to use something recognizable, such as numbers, for self-expression and art-making.

Molas of Panama

Ingredients:

- glue
- colorful strips of paper
- hole punch
- 12"x18" black paper
- craft scissors with a variety of blades
- die-cut nature shapes of various bright colors
- samples of Molas from Panama

Preparation:

Using a die-cut machine often found in schools, cut a variety of colors of papers into a variety of nature shapes. If you do not have access to a die-cutter, check an arts supply store, a craft or hobby store, or a teacher store for die-cut shapes. If the students can cut out their own nature shapes, have colorful paper scraps handy. Cut 1" wide strips of colorful paper.

Procedure:

Show the students the Molas of Panama. Ask them what they see. Molas are made of layers of colorful fabric pieces, often focused on nature. Demonstrate how to glue a variety of large nature shapes on the black paper. Demonstrate how to cut strips of paper with the craft scissors and layer the smaller pieces on top of the larger ones. Students cut nature shapes and glue them on the black paper. When the paper is full of large nature shapes, the students select strips of paper and craft scissors to cut smaller pieces of paper and glue them on top.

This activity provides the student with an opportunity to experience the art of another culture. It also facilitates an understanding of contrasting colors and overlapping.

Aboriginal Dot Paintings

Ingredients:

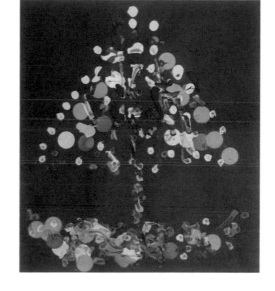

- black paper
- cotton swabs
- various colors of tempera paint
- pans
- colored dot stickers
- large stencils of animals, people or objects
- masking tape
- examples of Aboriginal Dot paintings

Preparation:

Cut the black paper to fit the stencils. Use masking tape around the edge of each stencil to attach it to a piece of black paper.

Procedure:

Introduce the Dot paintings of the Aboriginal people of Australia. Show examples and ask the students what they see.

Students select their stencil and attach some colored dot stickers on the black paper, within the stencil area. Demonstrate how to use the cotton swabs to dip and dot the colors on the paper, inside the stencil. Students use the cotton swabs to fill the stencil area with paint dots. Emphasize filling the edges of the shape. Remove stencil when dry.

This activity provides the student with an opportunity to experience the art of another culture while exploring color and pattern.

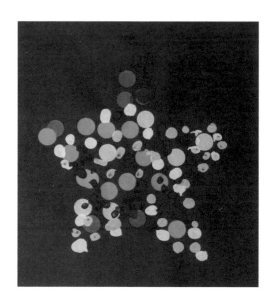

Rainbow Fish

Ingredients:

- white watercolor paper
- coloring supplies
- large fish-shaped stencils
- glitter paint in pans
- glue
- scissors
- aluminum foil pieces
- colorful sequins
- large paint brushes

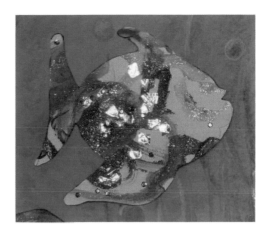

Procedure:

Read the book *Rainbow Fish,* by Marcus Pfister. Demonstrate how to draw a fish shape or students can use a fish-shaped stencil. Give each student a large piece of white watercolor paper and pencil. Students draw a large fish. Pass around pans of glitter paint, each color with its own brush. When dry, cut out the fish and glue on small pieces of aluminum foil and sequins. Reread the book and enjoy the beautiful fish.

This activity allows the students to make a connection between making art and book illustrations, while enjoying the sensory experience of painting with glitter paint.

Sculptural Hat

Ingredients:

- 3"x12" colored paper strips
- stapler
- paper crimper
- hole punches (variety of types)
- pipe cleaners
- feathers
- 1" lengths of plastic straws (thick type)
- yarn
- stickers
- colored tape

Important to note: This activity is intended for young children only. In order to preserve the dignity of students with disabilities it is always important to consider the age appropriateness of an activity.

Procedure:

Introduce the concept of sculpture and three-dimensionality. Look for sculptures or 3D objects in the room. The sculptures of Alexander Calder could be an inspiration for this artwork. Each student selects three strips of colored paper. Staple two ends together (stapling a few inches from the end will allow the hat to have paper stick out on the sides of the head making the hat even more fun). Staple another two ends together. Leave the third "corner" open so the strips can be crimped, if desired. Demonstrate how to crimp, punch holes, and string up yarn, straw pieces and paper scraps. Demonstrate how to bend and attach pipe cleaners and how to attach feathers with colored tape. Students attach whatever they want, decorating all surfaces, creating a sculpture for their heads. When finished, fit the hat to the student's head and staple the final side closed.

This engaging activity provides an opportunity to see how three-dimensional art interacts with the world around it.

Story Picture

Ingredients:

- 12"x12" colored paper and white paper
- 1"x12" matching colored paper strips
- crayons
- 8" square stencils
- diluted black tempera paint
- large brushes
- glue
- scissors
- pictures of pets
- white paper
- pencils

Procedure:

Introduce the concept of how a picture can tell a story. Show Winslow Homer's painting *The Herring Net*, or another artwork that is about stormy weather, and ask the students what they think is going on in the picture. Talk about stormy weather and ask about the color of the sky, lightning, etc. Demonstrate how to create a stormy sky using a white crayon for wind and a yellow crayon for lightning, and then brush the diluted black tempera paint over the crayon lines. Give each student a 12"x12" piece of white paper and have them create wind and lightning lines with white and yellow crayons. Give them the diluted black paint to brush over their crayon lines. Set aside to dry.

Each student selects a 12"x12" piece of colored paper. Students can draw independently or use a variety of stencils to create shapes, lines, and/or patterns on the colored paper, creating wallpaper for the interior of a house. Discuss windows – looking at the windows in the room, or thinking about windows at home. Show one of Henri Matisse's interior paintings and notice the window and wallpaper patterns.

Demonstrate how to place an 8" square in the center of the 12"x12" colored paper and trace around it. (This may require assistance.) Students trace and cut out an 8"x8" opening or window in the middle of their colored paper. Demonstrate how to glue the two matching colored strips across the back of the opening to create a window with four panes. With assistance, students build their windows and glue them down on top of their stormy sky paintings. Students draw a pet or select a pet picture to color, cut, and glue in the window. When finished, talk about what is happening in the picture. Ask questions about how the puppy might feel, how they feel when the weather is too bad to go outside.

This activity facilitates the understanding that a work of art can tell a story.

Day of the Dead Skeletons

Ingredients:

- 12"x18" black paper
- scissors
- glue
- 11"x17" black and white skeleton template
- miscellaneous decorations, such as: pompoms, sequins, fabric scraps, yarn, lace, ribbon, colored paper scraps, netting
- photos of Day of the Dead skeleton art

Preparation:

Create or find a black line drawing of a skeleton. If possible, allow the various limbs to be separate on the paper so the students can cut and build their skeletons in any manner desired.

Procedure:

Show artworks from Mexico's Day of the Dead celebration, and explain how the people of Mexico celebrate loved ones who came before them with this fun holiday and art. The students will enjoy these whimsical characters. Assist the students in cutting and building their skeletons. They do not have to be anatomically correct in their construction. Provide a selection of materials to "dress" the skeletons and assist with gluing as needed. This is a very fun project with humorous outcomes!

This activity allows the students to learn about the art of another culture and to discover that art can be humorous.

Andy Goldsworthy Nature Collages

Ingredients:

- pan of pea gravel
- collection of nature objects
- digital camera
- the art of Andy Goldsworthy

Preparation:

Collect shells, feathers and other objects that are not found around your school. Use silk flowers or leaves and they will last longer and will not turn into crumbs! Take the students for a walk around the school and collect a variety of nature objects.

Procedure:

Introduce the nature art of Andy Goldsworthy. Play "I Spy" and enjoy looking at his artwork. Give each child the opportunity to select any objects that they want to use and arrange them on the gravel in the pan. When they are finished, take a photograph of the nature collage. Allow the students to sort and return the objects to their bags or containers.

This activity connects art with nature and demonstrates that patterns can be found in nature.

Conclusion

When confidence is high and anxiety is low, students take risks (Ching, 1993). Through art, students with disabilities can comfortably participate in art activities that build on their cognitive and motor skills while providing opportunities for self-expression. The therapeutic benefits of art for all students, and especially for students with disabilities, give added importance to this area of the school curriculum. The lessons presented here just scratch the surface of possibilities for art activities that can be successfully presented to students with disabilities. These lessons will undoubtedly inspire new ideas for you and me. It is a place to begin thinking differently about art instruction. It has helped me to feel capable, confident and successful in my teaching practice and I hope it will do the same for you in whatever application suits your needs.

I do not see this as the conclusion but rather as the beginning for you and me. I am continually revisiting, revising and reinventing art lessons for my students. If you would like to contact me, I will gladly answer your email. I can be reached at makingartspecial@gmail.com.

Glossary

Here are some art terms found throughout the text that may need definition for some readers.

Abstract – changed, distorted or simplified work of art

Balance – symmetrical or asymmetrical arrangement of elements in a work of art

Brayer – ink roller used for making prints

Collage – attaching a variety of materials together on a surface

Cool colors – blue, green, purple

Contrast – differences in value, color, line, shape or texture

Emphasis –the focus or center of interest in a work of art

Movement – the suggestion of motion created in a work of art

Pattern – repeating shapes, colors or lines

Primary colors – red, yellow, blue

Proportion – relative size of parts to the whole

Rhythm – repeating movement of colors, shapes or lines

Secondary colors – orange, green, purple

Space – surface area or extent in two or three-dimensional work of art

Texture – the way something feels or looks like it feels

Unity – when all the elements in a work of art look like they belong together

Value – lightness and darkness of a color

Warm colors – red, yellow, orange

Index of Lessons

Additional Resources

Here are some resources that may be helpful.

Adaptive art suppliers:

www.infinitec.org/learn/art/artequipment.htm
www.bableto.com/
www.enasco.com/artsandcrafts/Cutting+Tools/Knives+&+Cutter
s/Adapt-A-Cut&%23174%3B/

Adaptive art supplier of OLO rolling scissors
www.artstuff.net/olo_rolling_scissors.htm

Advocacy organization www.disabilityisnatural.com/

American Art Therapy Association www.arttherapy.org

Art for the Blind www.artbeyondsight.org

Arts Edge www.artsedge.kennedy-center.org

Arts accessibility www.vsarts.org

Arts advocacy www.artpartnersprogram.com/

Autism www.autism-society.org

National Down Syndrome Society www.ndss.org

National Down Syndrome Congress www.ndsccenter.org/

National Institute of Art & Disabilities www.niadart.org/

National Institute on Deafness and Other Communication
Disorders Information www.nidcd.nih.gov

References

Edwards, B. (1979). *Drawing on the right side of the brain*. New York, NY: Penguin Putnam, Inc.

Ching, J.P. (1993). *Using art as a means of language development and of finding one's voice.* (ERIC Document Reproduction Services No. ED 373 351)

Gerber, B. L., & Guay, D. M. (2006). *Reaching and teaching students with special needs through art.* Reston, VA: National Art Education Association.

Henley, D. R., (1992). *Exceptional Children Exceptional Art*, Worchester, MA; Davis Publications Inc.

Kramer, E. (1971). *Art as therapy with children.* New York, NY: Schocken.

Krathwohl, D., Bloom, B., & Masia, B. (1956). *Taxonomy of educational objectives: The classification of educational goals. Handbook II: Affective domain.* New York: David McKay Co.

Lowenfeld, V. (1957). *Creative and mental growth.* 3rd edition. New York: Macmillan.

Passmore, K. (2005). Using the national standards to your best advantage. *School Arts*, 105(2), 48.

Striker, S. (2001). *Young at Art*. New York: Macmillan.

Tomlinson, C. (1999). *The differentiated classroom: Responding to the needs of all learners.* Alexandria, VA: Association for Supervision and Curriculum.

Tubbs, J. (2008). *Creative therapy for children on the Autism spectrum, ADD, and Asperger's*, Garden City Park, NY: Square One Publishers.

Wong, H. K., & Wong, R. T. (2004). *The first days of school.* Mountain View, CA: Harry K. Wong Publications, Inc.

Made in the USA
Lexington, KY
24 July 2011